Get Out of THE ALPHABET Number 2

Number 2

WACKY
WEDNESDAY
PUZZLE
POEMS

BY **Kalli Dakos**

PICTURES BY
Jenny Graham

Simon & Schuster Books for Young Readers

SIMON & SCHUSTER BOOKS FOR YOUNG READERS
An imprint of Simon & Schuster Children's Publishing Division
1230 Avenue of the Americas, New York, New York 10020
Text copyright © 1997 by Kalli Dakos
Illustrations copyright © 1997 by Jenny Graham
SIMON & SCHUSTER BOOKS FOR YOUNG READERS is a trademark of
Simon & Schuster.
Book design by Lucille Chomowicz
The text for this book is set in 14-point Mixage.
Printed and bound in Hong Kong by South China Printing Co. (1988) Ltd.
First Edition
10 9 8 7 6 5 4 3 2 1
Library of Congress Cataloging-in-Publication Data
Dakos, Kalli.
   Get out of the alphabet, Number 2! : wacky Wednesday
puzzle poems / by Kalli Dakos ; pictures by Jenny Graham.
          p.   cm.
   Summary: Ms. Churn's class makes up silly poems mixing up
letters and numbers.   ISBN 0-689-81118-7
   1. Alphabet—Juvenile poetry. 2. Numerals—Juvenile poetry.
3. Children's poetry, American. 4. Nonsense verses, American.
[1. School—Poetry. 2. Alphabet—Poetry. 3. Numerals—Poetry.
4. American poetry. 5. Nonsense verses.] I. Graham, Jenny (Jenny Mary),
ill. II. Title.PS3554.A414G48 1997 811'.54—dc20   96-19965

A Note from the Artist

I begin by sketching with a black marker on tracing
paper and when I find an image I like, I transfer it on
to the watercolor paper with a pencil. The final
illustrations for this book were painted with Windsor
and Newton gouache on 90 lb. Windsor and Newton
cold press watercolor paper.

*This book is dedicated to the memory of my father
and to the stories he told that enchanted my childhood*
—K. D.

For my father, Tony, and my husband, Peter
—J. G.

To Jane,
Good luck
with these wacky
poems!
Kalli Dakos
June 14, 1999

ABC

WACKY WEDNESDAY

Suzie: A B Z D E F G...

Tommy: You're saying the alphabet
All wrong!
It's A B C D E F G...

Suzie: You've forgotten
That today is a special day
In our school—
It's WACKY WEDNESDAY!

Richard: You CAN'T change the alphabet
Just because it's Wacky Wednesday.

Kristine: If you can wear
Your dad's underwear
OVER your pants today,
Then we can do
Whatever we want
With letters and numbers.
A B 3 D E F G...

Scottie: 3 isn't in the alphabet.
It's a number.

Kristine: Look at you!
You've got on
A purple hat
With jingle bells,
Just because it's Wacky Wednesday.
If you can do that,
I can put 3 in the alphabet.

Ariana: Wow!
This is fun.
Look what
I'm doing to G!
1 2 **G** 4 5 6 7 8 9

Ms. Churn: What a WACKY CLASS
I have this year.
I looooooooooooooooove
Your idea.
Hey, I have an idea
For a poem.
Give me a minute
To write it down,
And then see
If you can
Figure out
The wacky part.

GET OUT OF THE ALPHABET, NUMBER TWO

Get out of the alphabet,
Number 2.
We're too smart
To be fooled by you.

NAUGHTY NUMBER FOUR

Behave,
Behave,
Number 4,
Don't be naughty
Anymore.

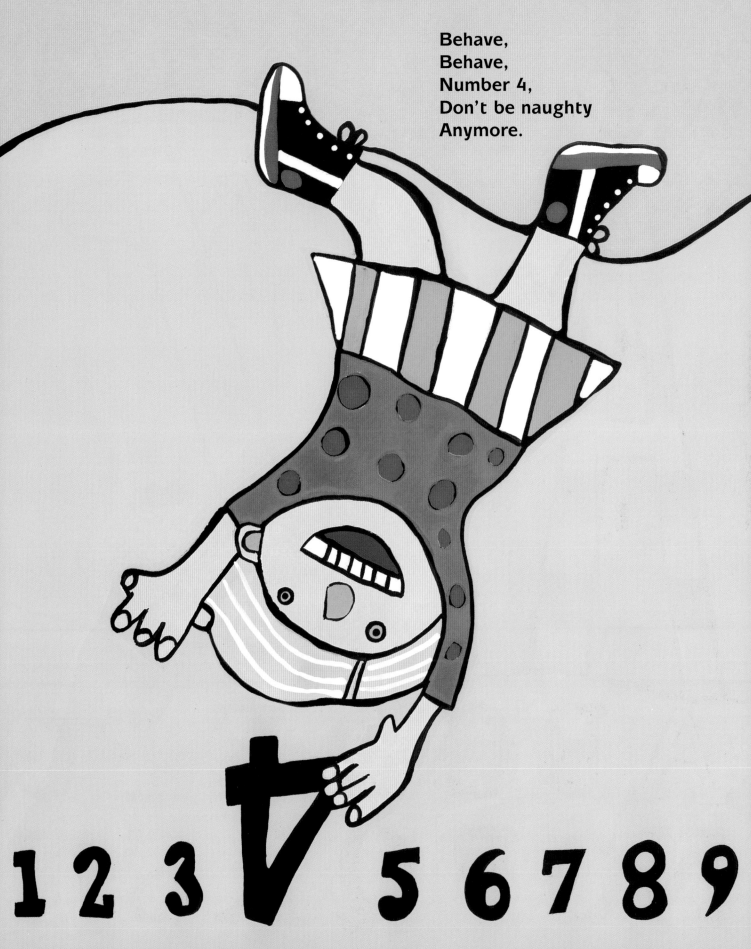

1 2 3 4 5 6 7 8 9

BE HAPPY

A and Z
Were in a fight
When S said,
"It is not right,

To fight about
Who is the best,
First or last,
East or west.

Number one
Or twenty-six,
It doesn't matter
How you mix.

Do not moan
Or whine or fret,
Be happy you're
The alphabet."

ABCDEFG
NOPQRST

WISH WE WERE YOU

First in the alphabet,
Best mark in school,
Sometimes the rest of us
Wish we were you.

H I J K L M
U V W X Y Z

STOP TALKING, PLEASE

Would you threes
Stop talking,
Please.

UPSIDE DOWN

He's really my twin,
But he acts like a clown,
Turn him right-side up,
Because he's upside down.

A LOT LIKE YOU

I think I look
A lot like you
And I should be
In the alphabet,
Too.

CUTE LITTLE DOT

i: i have this cute
     Little dot,
     Do you like it
     Or do you not?

r: i want a dot,
     i do, i do,
     i want a dot,
     Just like you.

ABCDEFGHIJKLMNPQRSTUVWXYZ

HOW DID YOU FORGET?

Oh,
How could it happen?
Oh,
How could it be?
Oh,
How did you forget
          ME?

Who is forgotten?

CAPITAL "I" ASKS CAPITAL "S" A QUESTION

I: I wish I was not
       So straight and firm.
       You are so curly,
       Did you get a perm?

S: No, I didn't,
       I was born this way.
       I think we *both*
       Look okay.

I DON'T WANT TO BE

P: I don't really
Want to be
The disgusting
Letter "P."

Z: All the letters
Have to be
What we're born,
And you're a "P."

P: Bathrooms, toilets,
Wait for me,
I refuse
To be a "P."

Z: Think of sweet, sweet
Summer peas
From the garden,
Letter "P."

P: Sweet peas,
Yes! I'll be!
I am the great
Letter "P."

Z: It's late
I'm tired,
Why must I be
The sleepy, sleepy
Letter Z Z Z Z Z z z z...

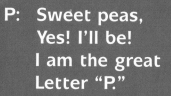

WWWWWWwww

STILL POWERFUL

No matter how little,
No matter how small,
We are still as powerful
As the big and the tall.

1 2 3 9 4 5 6 7 8 10

NAUGHTY NUMBER NINE ON THE WAY TO LUNCH

Number 9
Cut in line.

GET OUT OF THE CLOCK

What do you think
You're doing in there?

You have so much nerve!
How do you dare,

To take our place,
And think we don't care?

B o'clock, D o'clock,
We declare,

People won't understand,
Anywhere,

Get out of the clock,
You shouldn't be there!

KKKKKKKKKKKKKKKKKKKKKKKKKKKKKKKKKKKKKKKKKKKKKKKKKKKKKKKKKK
11111111111111111111111111111111111111111111111111111
22222222222222222222222222222222222222222
333333333333333333333333333333333
44444444444444444444444444444
55555555555555555555555
6666 3 66666666

I'M IN THE WRONG LINE

I'm in the wrong line,
In this brand new school.
The kids are too big,
And I look like a fool.

I've lost my new class,
And teacher, too.
Will someone tell me
What I should do?

6 6 6

1 2 3 4 5 6 7 9 10 8

YOU'RE ALWAYS LATE

Michael 8,
You're always late!

SCHOOL

1 2 3 4 5 6 7 9 10

SHOVING IN LINE

Z shoved in
Ahead of B,

And S jumped
In front of G,

And P ran to
Stand by V,

Mixed up alphabet,
You see.

ACDEFGHIJKLMNOPQRSTUVWXYZ

I DON'T LIKE YOU

I don't like you,
You're my enemy
Because one spring day
You stung me.
So in *my* alphabet
You will not be.

WE PLAYED WITH THE GLUE

At lunch we played with the glue,
Now we don't know what to do.

WE'RE BRAND NEW

We're brand new,
We're brand new,
And we want to be
In the alphabet, too.

Who is new?

LIKE U

u: When I grow up
Will I look like you?
U: You'll look like me,
I'll look like you,
You'll just be
A bigger U.

g: When I grow up
Will I look like you?
G: Gosh! Golly!
Whoa! Whoa! Whoa!
Your head and tail
Will have to go.

o: When I grow up
Will I look like you?
O: Round and fat
And chubby, too,
You're a smaller me,
I'm a bigger you.

1 2 3 4 5 6 7 8

1 2 3 4 5 6 7 8 9 10

ON THE WAY TO GYM

Number 9,
Get back in line!

ABCDEFGHIJKLmNOPQRSTUVWXYZ

DON'T PICK ME

Don't pick me,
Don't pick me,
Pleeeeeeeeeeeeeeeeeeeeeeeeeeeeeeeeeeeeeeease!
Pleeeeeeeeeeeeeeeeeeeeeeeeeeeeeeeeeeeeeeeeeeeeeeease!

Don't pick me.

Y?

P: I've played with a, e, i, o, and u,
   But I will not play with Y.

Y: Y?

P: Because you always
   Ask too many questions.

Y: Y?

P: That's Y.

A B C D E F
N O P Q R S

LET'S HAVE A PARTY

Alphabet: Come to our party,
We'll have so much fun.
You're all invited,
So come on the run.

Numbers: We're coming,
We're coming,
We'll bring a cake.
A party with you
Sounds perfectly great!

Alphabet: Someone came,
We didn't invite.
Do you think,
That's very polite?

1 2 3 4 5 6 7 8

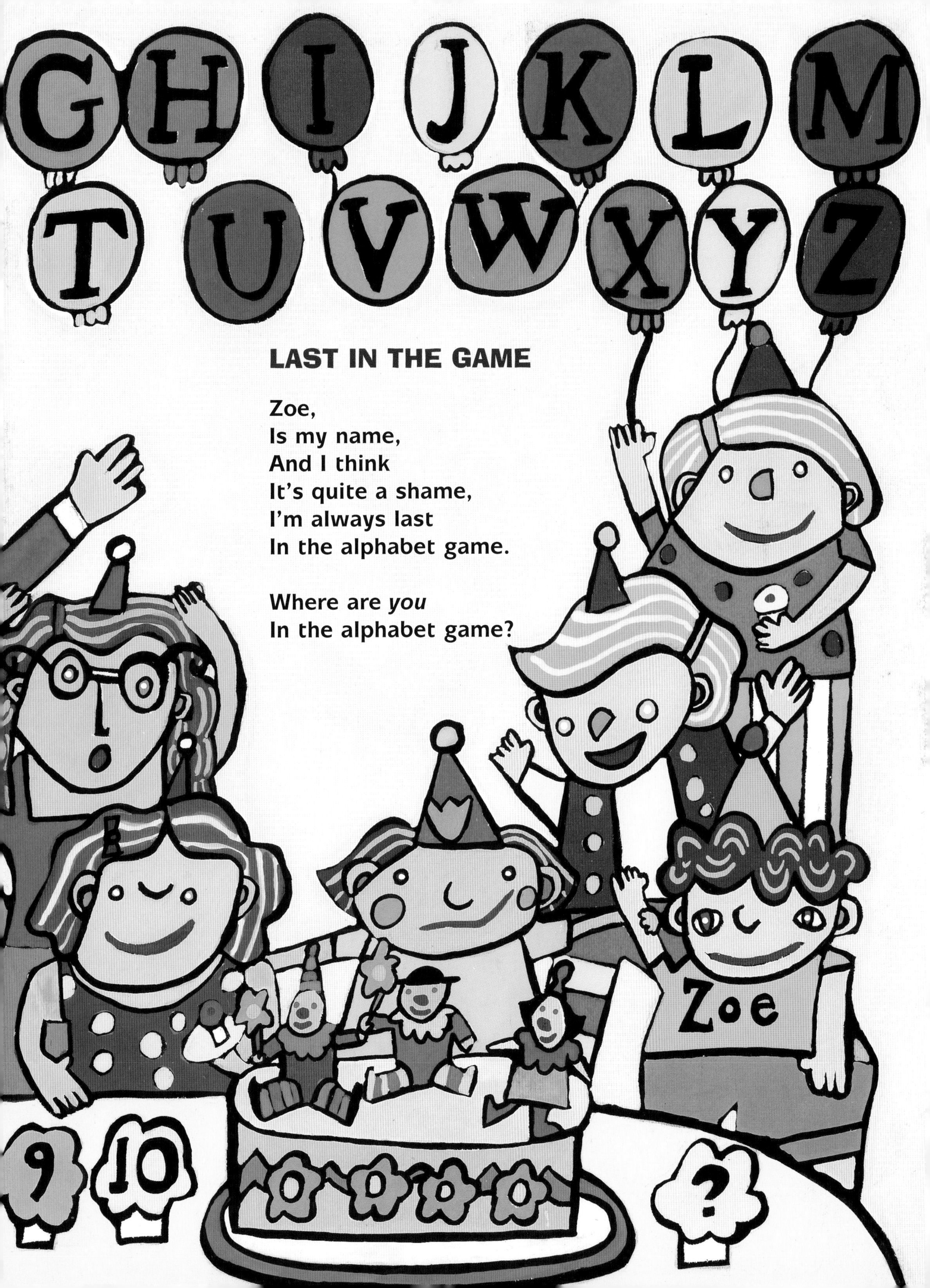

LAST IN THE GAME

Zoe,
Is my name,
And I think
It's quite a shame,
I'm always last
In the alphabet game.

Where are *you*
In the alphabet game?

2 3 4 5 6

1

TIME TO RETURN TO NORMAL

Ms. Churn: It has been a
Wonderful Wacky Wednesday!
But it is time
To return to normal.
The alphabet will go back to:

A B C D E F G H I J K L M N O P Q R S T U V W X Y Z

And the numbers back to:

1 2 3 4 5 6 7 8 9 10

Wacky Wednesday
Is officially over.
Please line up at the door.
And don't forget your book bags
And your homework,
It's D o'clock,
And time to go home!

0

7

8

9